On the Pitch

STARS OF WOMEN'S SOCCER

MEGAN COOLEY PETERSON

WORLD BOOK

This World Book edition of *Stars of Women's Soccer* is published by agreement between Black Rabbit Books and World Book, Inc.
© 2018 Black Rabbit Books,
2140 Howard Dr. West,
North Mankato, MN 56003 U.S.A.
World Book, Inc.,
180 North LaSalle St., Suite 900,
Chicago, IL 60601 U.S.A.

All rights reserved. No part of this book may be reproduced in any form without written permission from the publisher.

Marysa Storm, editor; Michael Sellner, designer; Omay Ayres, photo researcher

Library of Congress Control Number: 2016049978

ISBN: 978-0-7166-9345-1

Printed in the United States at CG Book Printers, North Mankato, Minnesota, 56003. 3/17

Image Credits

Alamy: INTERFOTO, 6–7; Jonathan Larsen/Diadem Images, 23 (Angerer); John Green / Cal Sport Media, 9, 10; Matt Jacques, 21; AP Images: EUGENE HOSHIKO, 1, 13 (Angerer), Back Cover; Getty Images: AFP / Stringer, 17; Christopher Morris, Cover; Elsa, 14; John W. McDonough, 24–25; NICHOLAS KAMM, 29; Newscom: Adam Davis/Icon Sportswire ASA, 23 (Leroux); ANDRE PICHETTE, 22 (Marta); Charles Mitchell/Icon Sportswire CFX, 22 (Morgan); Seth Sanchez/Icon Sportswire DDA, 19; Trask Smith, 18; Trask Smith/Cal Sport Media, 23 (Sinclair); Yusuke Nakanishi/AFLO, 22 (Sawa); Shutterstock: Dneprstock, 27 (cups); EKFS, 22–23 (stadium); Krivosheev Vitaly, 3, 15, 19 (background), 27 (background); makeitdouble, 28; SSSCCC, 16, 26–27 (net), 31; Vectomart, 6, 13 (soccer ball), 20, 26 (balls), 32; USA Today Sports: Jerome Miron, 4–5
Every effort has been made to contact copyright holders for material reproduced in this book. Any omissions will be rectified in subsequent printings if notice is given to the publisher.

Contents

CHAPTER 1
Finding the Net........5

CHAPTER 2
The Stars.............8

CHAPTER 3
Impressing Fans.....28

Other Resources...........30

CHAPTER 1

Finding the Net

A player **dribbles** the ball down the **pitch**. She dodges **defenders**. No one can stop her. She blasts the ball toward the goal. It soars into the net. The crowd goes wild.

Stars of soccer leave fans wanting more. Check out some of the game's biggest stars.

History of Women's Soccer

1881 The first *international* women's soccer game is played in Great Britain. Scotland beats England 3–0.

1895 British Ladies Football Club forms.

1921

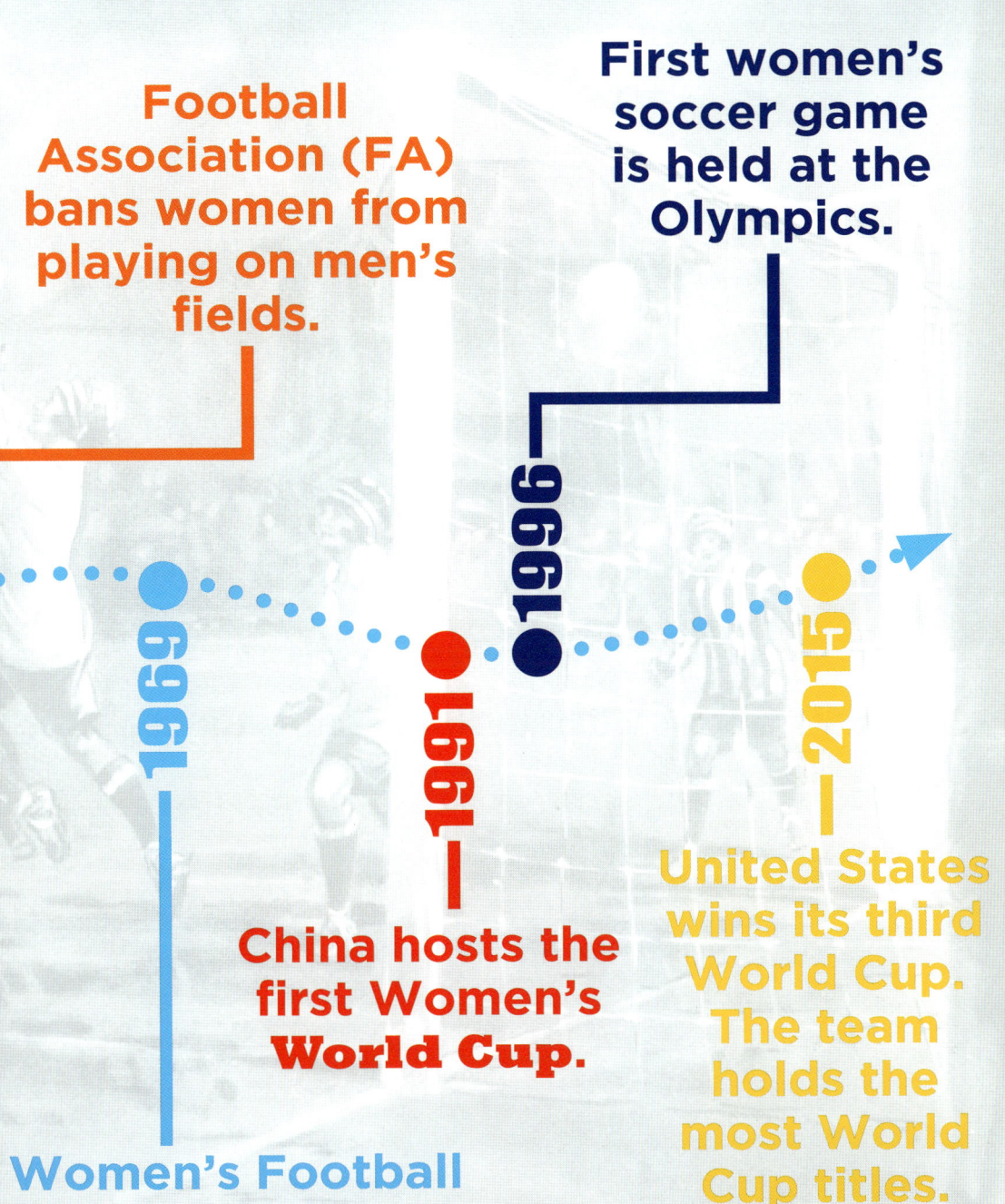

The Stars

Carli Lloyd

Carli Lloyd is a center **midfielder**. She can read the field better than most other players. She knows when to pass. She knows when to shoot. She is often the leading scorer for Team USA. Lloyd scored game-winning goals at the 2008 and 2012 Olympics.

In 2015, **FIFA** named Lloyd Women's World Player of the Year.

Marta

At the 2015 World Cup, Brazil's Marta took a **penalty** kick. Goal! This was her 15th career World Cup goal. She is the leading scorer in Women's World Cup history.

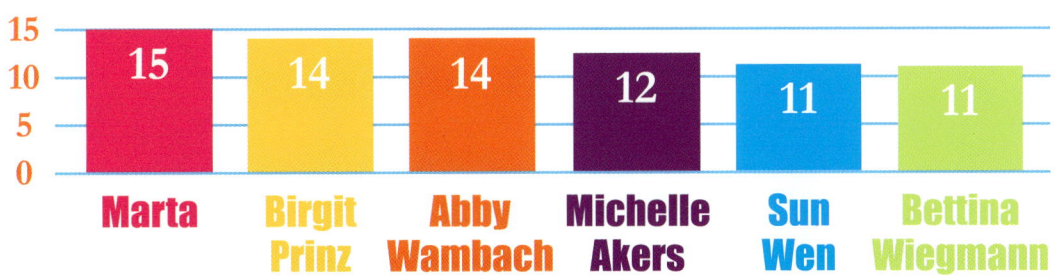

Nadine Angerer

Nadine Angerer was a German goalkeeper. Very few players could score against her.

In 2007, Germany went to the World Cup. Angerer set a record there. She did not allow a single goal during any of Germany's matches. Germany took the title. It beat Brazil 2–0.

FIFA World Players of the Year

Marta
2006, 2007, 2008, 2009, 2010

Birgit Prinz
2003, 2004, 2005

Mia Hamm
2001, 2002

Nadine Angerer
2013

Homare Sawa
2011

Abby Wambach
2012

Nadine Kessler
2014

Carli Lloyd
2015, 2016

14

Abby Wambach

Forward Abby Wambach was a scoring machine. She scored more **international** goals than any other player, male or female. She played for the United States.

At a 2010 match, Wambach split open her forehead. But she didn't leave the field. A doctor stapled the cut shut. She kept playing.

Homare Sawa

Homare Sawa played for Japan. She was a midfielder. Her quick moves amazed fans.

Japan played at the 2011 World Cup. The team was down one goal. Sawa scored! Her goal helped Japan win.

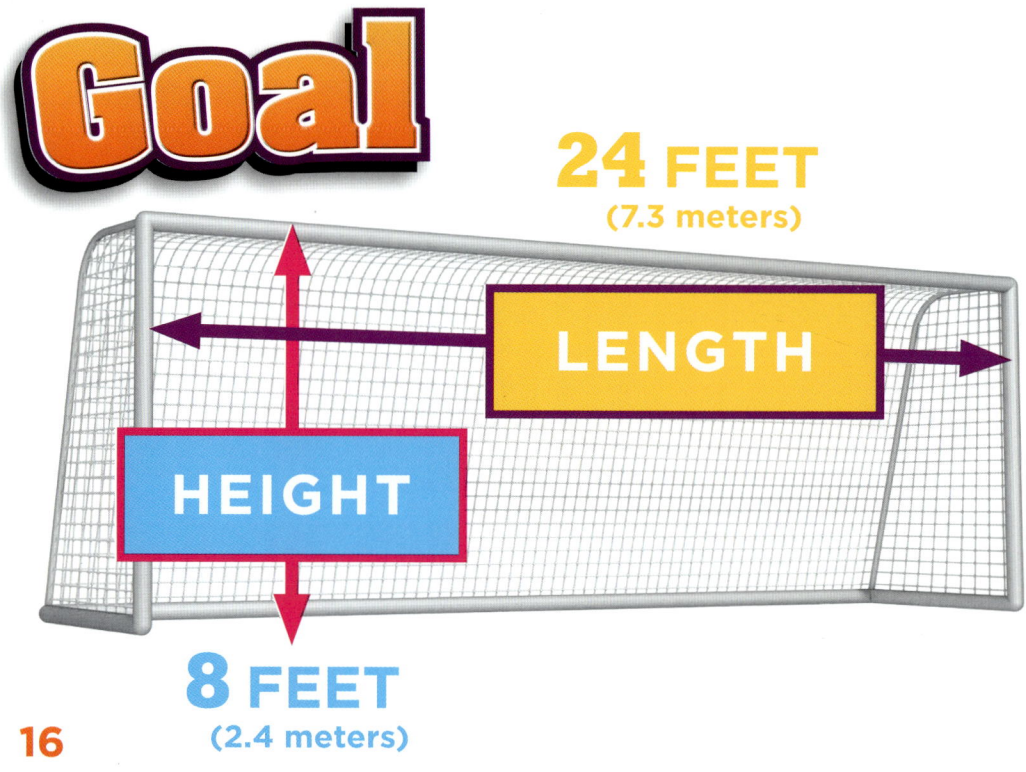

Christine Sinclair

Christine Sinclair plays for Canada. In February 2016, she scored her 161st international goal. The goal helped her team get to the Olympics. Fans can't wait to see what she does next.

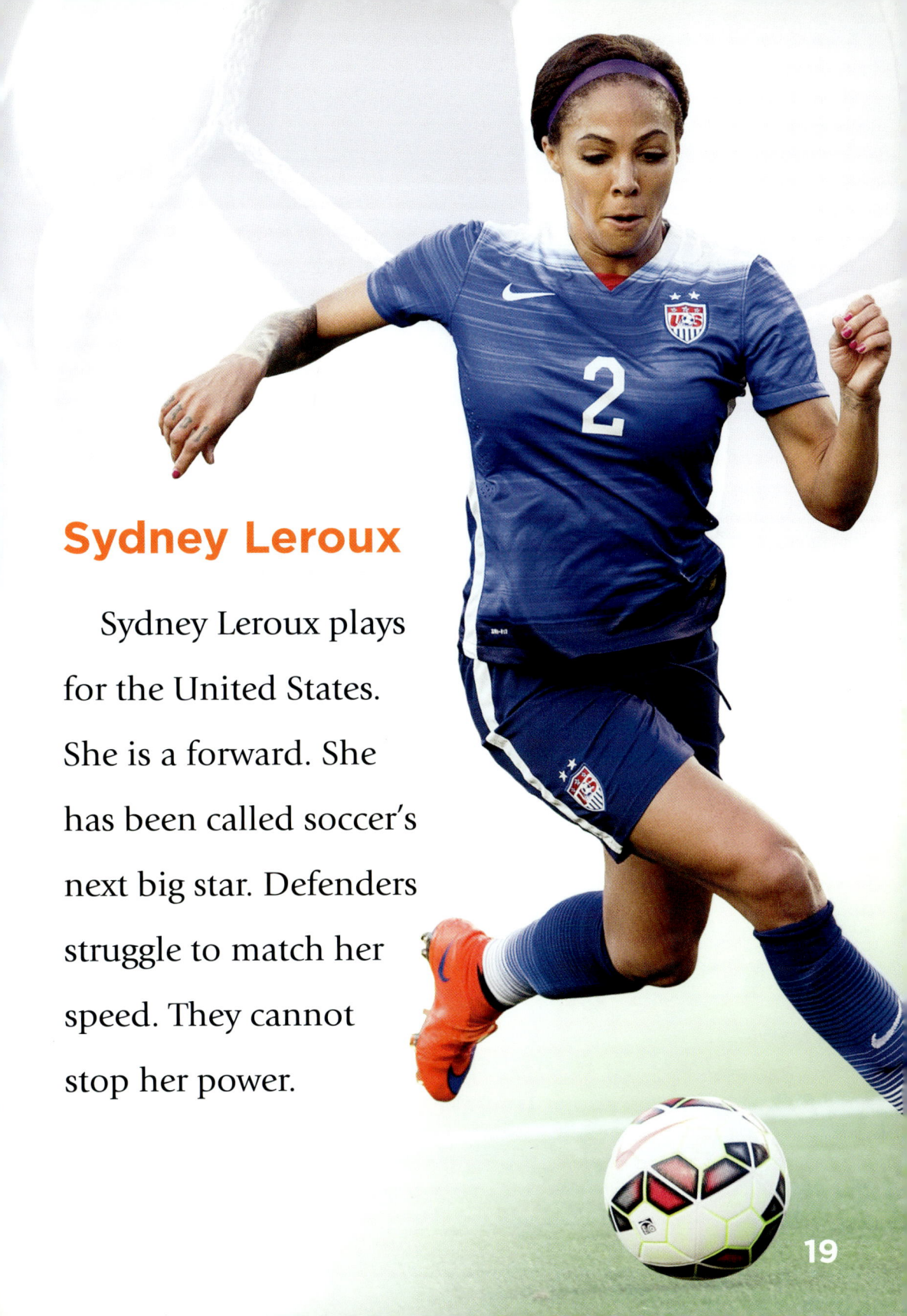

Sydney Leroux

Sydney Leroux plays for the United States. She is a forward. She has been called soccer's next big star. Defenders struggle to match her speed. They cannot stop her power.

Alex Morgan

Alex Morgan is a fast and high-scoring forward. She joined Team USA in 2009. At the time, she was the youngest player on the team. But she played like a pro. At the 2012 Olympics, she helped the team win gold. Morgan led the team to a 2015 World Cup win too.

In 2012, Morgan was Athlete of the Year. In 2013, she was Women's Player of the Year.

THE TALL AND SHORT OF IT

HEIGHT (inches)

- 64" (163 centimeters) — Marta
- 65" (165 cm) — Mia Hamm
- 65" (165 cm) — Homare Sawa
- 67" (170 cm) — Alex Morgan

22

Mia Hamm

Mia Hamm was a U.S. forward. Defenders swarmed her. But she was rarely stopped. She led the team to World Cup titles in 1991 and 1999.

The largest building at Nike headquarters is named for Hamm.

STARS OF THE WORLD CUP

World Cup Goals Scored

 = 5 goals

Marta — Brazil — 15

Mia Hamm — United States — 8

Abby Wambach — United States — 14

Birgit Prinz — Germany — 14

Homare Sawa — Japan — 8

World Cup Appearances

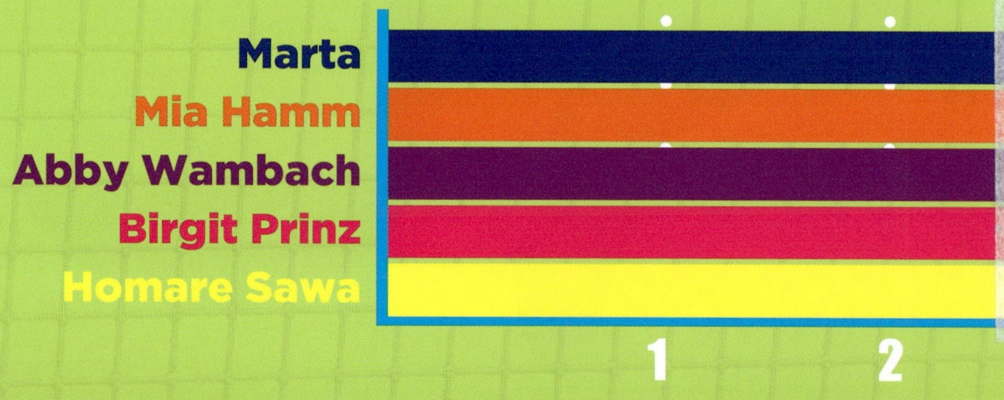

Player	Appearances
Marta	
Mia Hamm	
Abby Wambach	
Birgit Prinz	
Homare Sawa	

1   2

World Cup Titles

Marta 0

Mia Hamm 2

Birgit Prinz 2

Abby Wambach 1

Homare Sawa 1

Impressing

Soccer stars push the game to new heights. Their moves wow fans. Women's soccer stars are powerful players. They will keep fans thrilled for years to come.

GLOSSARY

defender (de-FEN-dur)—a player who works to stop the other team from scoring

dribble (DRI-buhl)—to move the ball along by kicking it with the feet

FIFA—International Federation of Association Football; FIFA controls world soccer.

forward (FOR-wurd)—a soccer player whose main job is to move the ball toward the opponent's goal and try to score

international (in-tur-NASH-uh-nuhl)—including more than one nation

midfielder (MID-feel-dur)—a soccer player who plays in the middle of the field; midfielders feed the ball to the forwards.

penalty (PEN-uhl-tee)—a punishment for breaking the rules

pitch (PITCH)—a soccer field

World Cup (WURLD CUP)—a soccer competition held every four years; teams from around the world compete against each other.

LEARN MORE

BOOKS

Fishman, Jon M. *Abby Wambach*. Amazing Athletes. Minneapolis: Lerner Publications Company, 2014.

Kortemeier, Todd. *Superstars of World Soccer*. Pro Sports Superstars. Mankato, MN: Amicus High Interest, 2017.

Murray, Laura K. *Alex Morgan*. The Big Time. Mankato, MN: Creative Education, 2016.

WEBSITES

FIFA Women's World Cup Canada 2015
www.fifa.com/womensworldcup/

Soccer (Football)
www.ducksters.com/sports/soccer.php

U.S. Women's National Team
www.ussoccer.com/womens-national-team

INDEX

A
Angerer, Nadine, 12, 13, 23

H
Hamm, Mia, 13, 22, 25, 26–27
history, 6–7

L
Leroux, Sydney, 19, 23
Lloyd, Carli, 8, 9, 23

M
Marta, 11, 13, 22, 26–27
Morgan, Alex, 20, 22

S
Sawa, Homare, 13, 16, 22, 26–27
Sinclair, Christine, 18, 23

W
Wambach, Abby, 11, 13, 15, 23, 26–27